# LES MISÉRABLES

FOR MUSICAL AND MOVIE LOVERS WHO
HAVE NOT READ VICTOR HUGO'S NOVEL

# LES MISÉRABLES

## FOR MUSICAL AND MOVIE LOVERS WHO HAVE NOT READ VICTOR HUGO'S NOVEL

Steve Antinoff

UNIVERSITYMEDIA
2012

Published by UniversityMedia, Wil / Paris / Philadelphia
www.universitymedia.org
Printed on acid-free and lignin-free paper

Library of Congress Cataloging-in-Publication Data
Antinoff, Steve, 1949–
    Les Misérables, for musical and movie lovers who
    have not read Victor Hugo's novel / Steve Antinoff.
    p.  cm.  — (UniversityMedia, Art & Religion)
    Includes bibliographical references and index
    ISBN 978–3–906000–18–3 (acid-free paper)
    1. Performing Arts—Musical—Les Misérables.
    2. Performing Arts—Film—Videos—Les Misérables.
    3. Victor Hugo (1813–1883).
    4. Fiction—France—19th century.
    5. Religion—Ethics—Art.
I. Title.

ISBN 978–3–906000–18–3

*To Richard DeMartino*

who gave and gave and gave

# Contents

# *Preface*

A contradiction of the 1980s is that what is commonly termed the "me generation" fell in love with a musical about a selfless man. All human beings, in experiencing the world, unavoidably find themselves as the center of their world. Self-centeredness therefore is tenacious. Yet Jean Valjean is beloved because there is in each of us an intimation that the highest form of self is to be selfless. We are moved to tears by selflessness, not by selfishness.

Why is that?

These pages are written for those inspired by the musical *Les Misérables* but who have not yet tackled Hugo's 1200-page masterpiece — for me, the greatest novel ever written.

The novel is pervaded by two central conflicts. The *first* is the conflict between love and justice. Love is championed by the bishop and, later, by Valjean. Justice is the supreme god of the fanatical Police Inspector Javert.

The *second* is the aforementioned conflict between love and egotism, and found within the heart of Jean Valjean himself. This second conflict is barely discernable in the Jean Valjean of the musical. Without it, he cannot be fully understood.

1

*Part One*

# A BISHOP BECOMES

# A CANDLESTICK

The fourth night after his release from prison Jean Valjean, having been refused lodgings everywhere else, even a dog kennel, is offered a meal and the first bed he has slept in for 19 years. His host, the Bishop of Digne — whose austere dwelling causes Valjean to mistake him for the local priest — notices that fear has prompted his housekeeper, Madame Magloire, to set the table minus the silver candlesticks reserved for guests. He gently requests the candlesticks be brought, along with the silver cutlery she has also withheld.

Awakening at 2 a.m., Valjean cautiously moves toward the never locked cupboard by the bishop's bed to steal "those silver knives and forks [that] obsessed him."[1] Misjudging the layout of the room in the darkness he unexpectedly bumps against his host's bed. Valjean tightens his grip on the sharpened spike in his hand. His gaze, writes Victor Hugo, was "terrifying."[D108] And yet — pausing — "Jean Valjean stood gazing in a kind of terror at the old man. He had never before seen anything like this." "This" means, of course, the sleeping face, which "wore a look of serenity, hope and beatitude."[D108]

---

[1] Victor Hugo, Les Misérables, trans. Norman Denny (London: Penguin, 1982), 105. The superscript letter D followed by a page number refers to this translation. The letter R with page number refers to the translation by Julie Rose (New York: Modern Library Paperback Edition, 2009).

*A terrifying gaze gazing in terror.* The paradox is crucial to understanding not only Valjean's encounter with the bishop but, 1000 pages later in a complete reversal, the existential collapse of Police Inspector Javert. Why would a beautiful old face terrorize a man?

## A film adds to the novel

In the 1978 English-language film version,[1] Madame Magloire had physically tried to prevent Valjean from even entering the house, shouting about "a monster [come] to murder us." The bishop finds such talk ridiculous and moves toward the door. His first words to Valjean are: "No one will hurt you here." It's a wonderful touch, making explicit the essence of the bishop. Hugo writes that with the exception of his mother and sister, Jean Valjean had never in his life encountered a friendly word or a kindly look. From the moment he arrives in Digne upon his release from prison, the townspeople, Madame Magloire included, are in fear of the harm he will cause them. The bishop's sole concern is to assure Valjean that no one will harm *him*.

In Victor Hugo's novel, Valjean announces himself as a felon, imprisoned for 19 years. The response is the invitation to stay the night. The kind welcome throws him. "A convict — and you aren't turning me out! You called me 'Monsieur.' 'Clear off, you dog,' is what they mostly say." [D85] He at least takes pride in having not concealed from the priest who he is. The bishop says it was unnecessary for Valjean to have explained anything. "This house

---

[1] This version features Richard Jordan as Valjean and Anthony Perkins as Javert. See page 84.

is not mine but Christ's. It does not ask a man his name but whether he is in need." "This is more your home than mine. Everything in it is yours. Why should I ask your name? In any case, I knew it before you told me." [D87] He then proves this to the startled Jean Valjean, saying: "Your name is my brother."

### The bishop before his collision with Jean Valjean

Such is the man who animates that face that terrorizes the terrifying Jean Valjean. We encounter this face as an accomplished fact, but of how it came to be the reader learns nothing. Unverified reports of the bishop's youth indicate he was a man of strong passions, even violence. His reasons for becoming a bishop are unknown. He married young but never abandoned extramarital affairs; he was groomed to inherit his father's position in the provincial parliament; the French revolution forced him to flee to Italy where his wife died having never borne children; he returned from Italy a priest. Hugo conjectures as a motive the reign of revolutionary terror of 1793, or the collapse of the old society or the downfall of his family, but offers an inner motivation as well that one gets the impression Hugo would prefer the reader to believe: "one of those mysterious and awful revulsions which, striking to the heart, change the nature of a man who cannot be broken by outward disasters affecting his life and fortune." [D19]

Three days after his assuming his post the bishop visits the tiny hospital next door, witnesses the cramped conditions, and decides to swap residences: he, his sister and their servant will live in the hospital; doctor and patients shall move into the bishop's palace. Of the bishop's yearly stipend of fifteen thousand francs, fourteen thousand go to charity. When, agitated by their financial difficulties, Madame Magloire convinces the bishop to apply for an additional three thousand habitually granted for carriage and travel expenses for tours of the dioceses, these too go to the poor, the bishop making his rounds either by foot, by cart, or by mule. To Madame Magloire's consternation, he refuses to lock their door. "If the devil walked into the house no one would prevent him," his sister writes in a letter. "He is afraid of nothing, even at night. That is his kind of courage, he says." [D47] How the Bishop acquired this courage we do not know.

### Valjean poised to murder the bishop

Jean Valjean, brutal, hate-filled from his unjust sentence and long years in prison, somehow does know, though semiconsciously, what in the bishop spawned "his kind of courage." It is this that terrifies him. Hugo writes that staring at the bishop's sleeping face no one, not Valjean himself, could have described his feeling. There is in this face a dimension of holy threat of which Valjean is "obscurely but strongly aware." [D108] It is a kind of preconscious intuition of the words spoken to Moses in Exodus (33:20) that no one can see the face of God and live. The beauty of the old bishop includes something lacking in the beauty of nature. In Somerset Maugham's novel *The Razor's Edge*, Larry Darrell, at the moment of his Enlightenment upon seeing the sun climb over a mountain lake in India, feels he is being killed by it. The bishop's beauty will also kill by the end of the day, but in a different way. The bishop's sleeping face, so beautiful to Valjean, also "horrified him," for it subjects Jean Valjean to a demand that nature alone, however awe-inducing, cannot set upon us: the demand to be human in the ultimate sense as in Abraham Heschel's: "Being human, I repeat, is inherent as a desideratum in human being."[1] This "desideratum" or demand, more than a cynical act of vengeance against the sole member of society who has treated Jean Valjean with goodness, is the reason why gazing into the sleeping face of the bishop he grips the spike more tightly in his hand. But it is also what stays his hand. It is both. "He was in a state of strange indecision, seemingly adrift between the two extremes of death on the one hand and salvation on the other — ready to shatter that skull or kiss that hand." [D108] Jean Valjean removes his hat, lets his arm fall, and looks on at the bishop for several minutes, both arms at his side, in one hand the sign of his reverence, in the other the instrument of murder. Finally he turns from the bishop, steals the silver from the cupboard, and hurries out.

*Love versus Justice:*
*The first of the two great dilemmas of Les Misérables*

The morning after he steals the silver, Jean Valjean is brought back in police custody to the bishop's house. He hears the man he thought was but a humble priest addressed by the police as "Monseigneur." He has robbed a bishop! The bishop is probably too unworldly to know that a second conviction for Valjean while on parole car-

---

[1] Abraham Heschel, *Who is Man?* (Stanford: Stanford University Press, 1965), 17.

ries the penalty of life imprisonment. What he does know, from the horrendous suffering in Jean Valjean's face, is what a return to prison would mean: the justice to which the bishop is entitled as the victim of the theft will entail for Valjean his spiritual destruction. At the moment the arm of justice is about to destroy Jean Valjean with no less force than hours earlier Valjean himself was prepared to use to drive the sharp spike into the bishop's skull, his victim ignores his right to justice and lies to the police. With the bishop's lie — that the stolen silver was a gift — the demands of justice are set aside in the name of love. On that loving lie Jean Valjean is redeemed. From then on, the entangled relationship between love and justice becomes one of two radii around which *Les Misérables* revolves. For Jean Valjean, transformed by love into a man of love, is to be hunted into old age by the fanatical man of justice, Javert. And should it be thought that the issue is simple and that love need only supplant justice to save and to heal (as the bishop's supplanting of justice with love saves and heals Jean Valjean), should it be thought that love is invariably greater than justice and worth more, let the reader hold this in the back of the mind: At the most critical point in his profound, undying love for his "daughter" Cosette, Jean Valjean's love is unjust, on the verge of destroying her happiness and her beloved Marius's life.

### The bishop forms a cross

There could be no *Les Misérables* without this scene in which the bishop lies to the police and yet Victor Hugo, the author of this novel of over 1200 pages, deals with it in little more than one page. The excessive Hugo —

who spends sixty-nine pages in small printed French on a military battle of which only the last seven have anything to do with the story, fifty pages on an irrelevant discussion of religious orders and monasteries, and many paragraphs on details of Paris underworld slang — devotes a single page to the foundational scene of his massive edifice, a scene in which the hero of his story speaks a dozen words. This is no accident. The bishop in the horizontal continuum of Jean Valjean's life from birth to death occupies no more than twelve hours, but he cuts vertically against that continuum both instantaneously and eternally, and in the fact and nature of that cutting lies his whole significance.

The policemen that bring Jean Valjean back to the bishop with the silver in his knapsack say he "seemed to be on the run."[D111] Leaving again a free man, knapsack filled with the same silver plus the two silver candlesticks the bishop falsely said Jean Valjean had forgotten, he is again described as having "left the town as though he were still on the run." [D112] Same man, same sack stuffed with silver, same actions. To a bystander viewing both flights they would seem to be interchangeable. But what threatened Jean Valjean as he ran from the scene of the robbery was at his heels; as he runs from the bishop's lie, what threatens him is at his toes. The bishop, I reiterate — as it is *the* defining factor of every subsequent second of Valjean's life — cuts against him vertically, vertically and eternally, and Jean Valjean charges into him — and the demand he represents — at each step.

*Unlike in the musical, a new theft, not just the bishop's forgiveness, causes Valjean's redemption*

Hugo writes that Valjean after departing from the bishop was angry, without knowing at whom; that at moments he wished himself back in prison and that these events had not happened to him; that the day was spent in growing turmoil; that he ran through the countryside blindly, not realizing he was going around in circles. By evening he is seated on the ground by a thicket in a deserted plain. The form of the verb is crucial. "He was seated," not: "He sat." In the legend of the life of the Buddha, the dissatisfied ex-Prince Gautama, six years after fleeing his palace in search of liberation from old age, sickness, and death, reaches the existential limit of despair, his quest for freedom having proved entirely useless. Out of moves, he sits in a deserted spot under a tree. That sitting is not simply an act of will; it is the exhaustion of will. He cannot take one further step. His sitting is the final act; he will either rise as a liberated man or he will die there. In Zen Buddhism this impasse is considered the mandatory precondition for Enlightenment. One must be existentially blocked at all points of the compass, no longer able to move forward, retreat, or maintain one's position. It is likened to a man on the tip of a hundred foot pole who is required to take a further step. It is likened to a man clinging by his teeth to a branch hanging over a precipice who is required to answer a question. It is likened to a man in a stupor, not knowing he is standing when standing, or sitting when sitting. It has been described (by the Zen master Shin'ichi Hisamatsu) "in terms of the intellect, as absolute contradiction; in terms of the emotions, as absolute agony; in terms of the will,

12

as absolute dilemma;" and it is clear that Hugo has intuited the dynamics of spiritual transformation along these lines. Jean Valjean's crisis with the bishop "had dazed him spiritually." [D116] When the bishop tells the police they were mistaken in assuming a theft, Valjean mumbles his few words of response "as if he were talking in his sleep," and receives the gift of the silver candlesticks from the bishop's hands "mechanically and with a distracted air." When the police withdraw "Valjean stayed motionless as though he were on the verge of collapse." [D111] He leaves the bishop "in a state of mind unlike anything he had ever experienced before and was quite unable to account for what was taking place within him." [D115] He is "plunge[d] ... into a state of agonized and almost intolerable confusion." [D116]

It is in this state, seated by the undergrowth in the twilight, that he encounters a character not in the musical, the itinerant child chimney sweep Petit-Gervais, singing as he walks along the footpath flipping his coins and catching them on the back of his hand. He stops by the thicket without noticing Valjean, fails to catch his largest coin, a piece worth forty cents. It rolls toward Valjean who slams his foot on it. The boy makes repeated attempts to retrieve the coin. Valjean fluctuates from the rudest insistence that the boy scram to an intermittent trance in which he seems unable to see or hear, and from which he finally emerges only to reach for his stick and cry out in a terrified: "Who's there?"

Suddenly he stands, his foot on the coin. Frightened, the boy runs off. No sooner is he gone than Valjean is absorbed again in his motionless stupor, until well into the evening the chill returns him to consciousness and,

13

reaching for the stick, he notices the coin, half buried by his foot. "It affected him like an electric shock." [D114] He picks up the coin, starts to walk, then to run into the desolate night screaming the child's name. Thus Jean Valjean, with more wealth in his knapsack than in all the days of his life added together, for a coin worth a few cents, becomes a "recidivist felon," a second-time offender who if convicted must be returned to prison for life. Why had he stolen it? "Assuredly he could not have answered the question." [D117] His legs buckle under him "as though some unseen power had struck him down" [D115] and he weeps convulsively, the first tears since an iron collar was riveted round his neck nineteen years earlier. "The fact is — a strange phenomenon, only conceivable in the situation he had found himself — that in robbing the boy he had committed an act of which he was no longer capable." [D117] His shock that he has robbed the boy precipitates Valjean's transfiguration, catalyzed by the bishop's forgiveness.

### Valjean *in*human
#### (or why no feline has ever been *in*cat)

Hugo writes that the prison term of nineteen years that Jean Valjean serves for stealing bread for his sister and her seven starving children turns him into an animal. But while a human being can sink lower than an animal, it can never be solely animal, and Hugo knows this well. When at the end of Franz Kafka's *The Trial* Joseph K. judges that he is about to die: "Like a dog!" — it is not the death a dog dies or the life a dog lives that he is judging. Jean Valjean's "animality" is what it can never be for an animal — a Fall. To be "a pig," to have "acted like a beast," to die "like a dog," are words of condemnation only for that being capable of violating its humanity. No animal violates itself. Only in being human, as distinct from being non-human, can being human, as distinct from being inhuman (or inhumane), be a matter on which the worth of an existence rises or collapses.

So when four days after his release from prison (having failed to find even a glass of water at the inn, having failed to find an hour's sleep even in the local prison, even in a kennel) Jean Valjean cries out: "I'm not even a dog!" — it is an expression, however negative, of human spirituality. Hugo is profound in saying that "during those nineteen years of torture and enslavement his spirit both grew and shrank." [D98] His is a spirit capable of what no animal can do: hating the world in its entirety and hating the God who created it. Prison having certain affinities to monastic life, there is already something religious in his hatred — priestly, ascetic, world-transcending because world-denying, renouncing pleasure, renouncing love. Barely educated, Jean Valjean has none of the sophistication of an Ivan Karamazov who, as Camus writes, puts God on trial on moral grounds. He has no intellectual arguments, and relies solely on his hatred. Even when at forty he learns to read in prison it is on the principle that an improved mind will make him a better hater. The hugeness of spirit so evident later in the story is already forged in prison, albeit in a perverted and "shrunken" form capable of expressing itself only in embittered revenge. That is the reason Hugo can claim of Valjean that "only [the bishop] could have overshadowed" him; [D118] only a power as mighty as the bishop's could have undermined his own. The bishop would have failed to transform a lesser spiritual negativity, just as Jean Valjean will later fail to transform Javert.

That theirs will be a battle to the death is intimated clearly enough. Shortly before the robbery, by the light of the silver candlesticks, the bishop shows Valjean to his bed in the room next to his. "Sleep well," the bishop says. "Before you leave tomorrow you must have a bowl of warm milk from our cows." Valjean thanks him, then adds menacingly: "This is wonderful! You're putting me to sleep in a bed next to your own. Have you thought what you're doing? How do you know I have never murdered anyone?" The bishop replies quietly: "That is God's affair." D91

Hugo describes the laughter that accompanies Valjean's threat as "monstrous." The serene detachment of the bishop is the only force this universe makes available to men and women that can undercut the power to murder where the victim is unwilling to resist with physical force of his own. The old man raises his hand gravely in benediction, two fingers extended to Jean Valjean. Valjean rejects it, refusing to bow his head. Without looking back he goes to his room. Two boxers: one prepared to go for the kill, one whose greatest weapon is his willingness to be killed. When Jean Valjean sees the bishop next, it is at his bedside with the spike in his hand.

*Altering God's Commandments*

To repeat, Jean Valjean is not transformed at the moment he is set free by the bishop, only plunged into a stupefied impasse caused by the opposition of forces within him. Outwardly, as we have seen, he is running about the countryside in circles, inwardly he tries to harden himself against what the bishop had done and said. Above all "he sought to suppress" [D116] the bishop's final utterance. "Do not forget, do not ever forget, that you have promised me to use the money [from the sale of the silver] to make yourself an honest man ... Jean Valjean, my brother, you no longer belong to what is evil but to what is good. I have bought your soul to save it from black thoughts and the spirit of perdition, and I give it to God." [D111]

*Valjean had made no such promise.* When the bishop says he had made it, Valjean remains silent. Yet the vehemence of his attempts to deny the promise after leaving the bishop for the last time reveals his hidden greatness. It is the first magnificence of Jean Valjean that hideous, hating, utterly degraded, he elevates the promise to be an honest man — which he did not even make — from "Thou shalt not steal!" and from "Thou shalt not bear false witness!" to "Love thy neighbor as thyself!" No one forced that upon him, not even the bishop.

That was his own doing, and his undoing. Marvelousness explodes from the bowels of this monster, seizing the story of Diogenes — lantern in hand, hunting the streets of Athens for an honest man — and transfiguring the meaning of "honest man" to the loftiest human possibility. It is a titanic act of spiritual imagination, albeit semiconscious, almost inconceivable for a being so downtrodden. From his own vision Valjean shrinks back, somehow apprehending that a truly honest life means a hell far greater than anything experienced in prison, which is why Hugo writes that Jean Valjean "obscurely ... perceived that the priest's forgiveness was the most formidable assault he had ever sustained." [D116] But at no point until his dying breath is he willing to define the promise in less uncompromising terms. He tries to defile it, to deny that the promise is binding on his existence. Yet he will not redefine it more lightly. "He must either conquer or be conquered, … the battle was now joined, a momentous and decisive battle between the evil in himself and the goodness of that other man." [D116]

It was his vow upon his release from prison that he would sink as low as humanly possible. Destroying the power of the promise would be the ultimate expression and fulfillment of that vow. He would kill it if he can. If he cannot, it would force him to become — against himself — what Javert — also against himself — is forced in the moments before his suicide to say of Jean Valjean: "a man near to the angels." [D1106] It explains why Valjean hungered to kill the bishop. Failing to do so, he gives the old priest his fatal chance. Forgiveness transmutes the bishop into the candlesticks, into an eternal demand. That is why Jean Valjean runs from, and into, the bishop; why, Hugo writes, "Henceforth there could be no middle way for him, … he must become either the best of men or the worst, rise even higher than the bishop himself or sink lower than the felon, reach supreme heights of goodness or become a monster of depravity." [D116]

The shock of the coin under his foot drags Valjean against the fact that despite himself, against his will, the promise *has* been made. The candle, far from being extinguished, extinguishes him.

> Thus he contemplated himself, as it were face to face, and there arose in his vision, at some mysterious depth, a sort of light resembling that of a torch. But as he looked more closely at this light

growing in his consciousness he saw that it had a human form and that it was the bishop.

His mind's eye considered these two men now presented to him, the bishop and Jean Valjean. Only the first could have overshadowed the second. By a singular process special to this kind of ecstasy, as his trance continued the bishop grew and gained in splendour in his eyes, while Jean Valjean shrank and faded. A moment came when Valjean was no more than a shadow, and then he vanished entirely. The bishop alone remained, flooding that unhappy soul with radiance.

Jean Valjean wept for a long time, sobbing convulsively with more than a woman's abandon, more than the anguish of a child. And as he wept a new day dawned in his spirit, a day both wonderful and terrible. He saw all things with a clarity that he had never known before — his past life, his first offence and long expiation, his outward coarsening and inward hardening, his release enriched with so many plans for revenge, the incident at the bishop's house, and this last abominable act, the robbing of a child, rendered the more shameful by the fact that it followed the bishop's forgiveness. He saw all this, the picture of his life, which was horrible, and of his own soul, hideous in its ugliness. Yet a new day had now dawned for that life and soul; and he seemed to see Satan bathed in the light of Paradise. D117-8

# Part Two

# THE CROSS OF

# JEAN VALJEAN

From the day of the robbery of the wandering chimney sweep Petit-Gervais, Jean Valjean's life has been governed by two aims: "to conceal his true identity, and sanctify his life ... and [to] find his way back to God. The two considerations were so closely linked as to be inseparable in his mind, both so absorbing and overriding as to govern his every act." [D209] In their pursuit he at once "contrived to vanish, sold the bishop's silver, keeping only the candlesticks as a reminder." [D208] Working his way across France under the alias Monsieur Madeleine (derived from Mary Magdalene) he arrives in Montreuil-sur-mer, teaches the populace a cheaper way of manufacturing its sole industry of glass beads at half the price, enriches the town as well as himself and in gratitude — though he tries to refuse the post — is appointed mayor. He invests much of his profits in the town, expands the hospital, builds schools, gives pennies to children, performs his official duties as mayor yet beyond that keeps to himself.

But *Les Misérables* is at its core the slaying of the illusion that the self-preservation Madeleine seeks through concealment, and the life of loving virtue he aspires to once the bishop "buys his soul," can survive as a unity — despite his attempt to achieve them both through a single path. It is not merely that accidents of human destiny such as the arrival of Javert as Montreuil-sur-mer's police inspector split that path in opposing directions.

Had Madeleine not worked in the same town as Javert, he would no doubt have lived out his life in goodness and safety, but to "find his way back to God" is a far more merciless affair. Judaism offers that when the dead Baal Shem Tov, founder of Hasidism, came to his son in a dream and his son asked: "What is faith?" he at once appeared on the top of a mountain and leapt into an abyss.[1]

*The first cross of Monsieur Madeleine:*
*only Jean Valjean could lift this cart*

Just how merciless his road to God is becomes clear in a moment of high moral beauty. A cart, sinking steadily into the mud, has fallen on old Fauchelevent, a businessman gone bust and one of the few persons in the town hostile to Madeleine. He is caught between the wheels, the whole weight of the cart crushing his chest, dying. Madeleine, happening on the scene, offers five, then ten, then twenty gold pieces for someone to climb under the cart and lift it with his back.

"It's not that we don't want to," says a voice. Madeleine turns and recognizes police inspector Javert. "It's a question of strength. You need to be tremendously strong to lift a load like that on your back," Javert continues. His eyes are fixed on the mayor. "I have known only one man, Monsieur Madeleine, capable of doing what you ask." Madeleine flinches. Javert adds casually, "He was a convict. In Toulon prison." [D169]

The mayor turns pale. The pinned man screams for

---

[1] Elie Wiesel, *Souls on Fire: Portraits and Legends of Hasidic Masters* (New York: Random House, 1972), 52.

help. Madeleine repeats his offer of twenty pieces of gold; Javert restates his assertion that only the convict he has mentioned is capable of doing what he asks. The man screams again. Madeleine looks around at the paralyzed bystanders and — compelled by love to an act that may expose his identity — smiles sadly. Without another word he is on his knees and under the cart. He raises the wheels from out of the muddy quagmire; the onlookers gain courage to pitch in and Fauchelevent is pulled out. As the old man clasps him around the knees and blesses him, Madeleine's expression bears "an indescribable mingling of distress and triumph." [D170] Finally he looks calmly at Javert, who meets his gaze with equal calm and a lot more hardness.

### A bit of Thénardier hiding in the mayor?

There one saw the full force of a man transformed by what the theologian Reinhold Niebuhr called one of the fundamental qualities of grace — *grace as power*: a human being completed by an infusion of divine power enabling him to love far beyond what the individual in its egotism could do on its own. One likewise saw Javert, infused by an equally divine power — justice — but a justice in which the love infusing Madeleine was missing, and understood why Hugo in writing of Javert says the absolute dedication to a good could be hideous. One saw in the sad smile the radiance of Madeleine's loneliness, caught as he was between the screams of the crushed old man and the threat pouring from Javert. One saw Madeleine move toward the cart and do what we would all long to do in that situation, and probably would not have done before Javert, even if we had the strength.

But there was Madeleine's turning pale at the mention of Toulon prison. There was the hesitation in response to the old man's screams. There was the look of triumph, which implied the existence of powerful forces of resistance in Madeleine's heart that had needed to be subdued — meaning that putting himself under the cart had been a victory of will rather than a love wholly natural to him, and that selfishness might in turn triumph were the risk to the mayor more acute. Then you knew that Jean Valjean had been right to shrink back from the bishop's forgiveness, that it was indeed "an assault" that could terrorize a soul as great as Jean Valjean's to wish that he were back in prison. That the greater the person the greater the terror, so that it posed a far deeper threat to Jean Valjean in his goodness than it would to the innkeeper Thénardier in his evil; for had Thénardier been forgiven the theft of the silver and been given the candlesticks he would have said: "Thanks, sucker!" and had he been told by the bishop he'd had made a promise would have added, "Sure, pal, you bet!" and blithely moved on.

These red flags were minuscule, dwarfed by Madeleine's lifting the cart, and then — with torn clothes, covered with mud, soaked in sweat — looking calmly at Javert. Warnings too covert not to be obscured by the mayor's selfless magnificence. But signals, nonetheless, that the imagined oneness of love and self-preservation, if tested at the ultimate point, might be blown apart into a thousand shards.

*The second cross of Monsieur Madeleine:*
*Conclusion #1: So nice to have God on your side*

Blown apart in one of the most moving episodes in all art. Javert walks into Madeleine's office demanding to be fired for a serious breach of discipline. Six weeks before, after the quarrel over the prostitute Fantine's prison sentence,[1] he had denounced the mayor to the Prefect of Police in Paris, accusing him of being the ex-convict Jean Valjean, wanted on new charges of robbing a small boy eight years earlier. Paris has reported back that Javert is mad, for the real Jean Valjean has been caught. He will be tried and convicted the next day and, as a repeat offender, sentenced to prison for life. Madeleine refuses Javert's request for dismissal. Javert is disgruntled. He, having lived by and for justice, has been unjust to a figure of authority; justice must be now brought against himself. Madeleine responds with a mere: "We'll see." Javert departs, announcing he will stay on his post until a replacement is found, and Madeleine is left to crash into his solitude.

The collision turns his hair white in a single night. The dizzying element in the crisis that now tightens around Madeleine is that he is essentially free, that his salvation or damnation depend finally not on Javert's report of the mistaken arrest or any other external circumstance but on his own free decision. For eight years, we are told, he has shuddered at the prospect of hearing the name Jean Valjean, only to find, now that the name has come to the fore, it poses "no threat unless *he* chose to make it so." [D211] What he feared most will actually save him; all he need

---

[1] See in Part Three the section entitled "A cop and a mayor volley over Fantine" (pp. 43–44) for an account of this dispute.

do is sit back and do nothing for twenty-four hours. True, circumstances have pushed him to the precipice; but if faith indeed be a plunge into the abyss there is a substitute in perfect position to take the fall: a stranger, one for whom Valjean bears no emotional tie. "It came to this: that his place in prison was still vacant, rendered vacant by his robbery of the boy, that it was empty and awaiting him and would continue to claim him until he returned to it, and that this was inexorable." And since "someone had to go into the chasm, he or another," why not "let things take their course" so that it will be the other? D212

Thus what Madeleine dreamed of and prayed for nightly will be his: "perfect security." D213 With the case wrapped up and the "real Valjean" in prison Javert will be off his trail, gone somewhere to be a field laborer as he himself had said in penitence for his affront to the mayor. Madeleine will be ever more honored as a benevolent man, and of course he *will* be benevolent. Surely all this has been ordained by God, willed by God because he wishes Madeleine to carry on "do[ing] good in the world and to set an example to other men, to let it be seen that the way of virtue and repentance is not divorced from happiness." D213 "It is not for me to oppose the will of God." D213

Such are the conclusions of Madeleine, and their power resides in their coming not from an evil and unworthy man, but from an astonishingly good one. "Certainly it would have been a great thing if, following the bishop's solemn admonition, after the years of repentance and self-denial and in the full flood of a rehabilitation so well begun, he had not faltered even in the face of this fearful dilemma but had steadily pursued the course towards the abyss in the heart of which lay spiritual salvation; it would have been a great thing, but it did not happen ... The first victor was the instinct of self-preservation." [D209-10]

### A second conclusion crosses out the first

Subjected to this test, a force latent in his own sublime nature breaks forth in Madeleine, a force that cannot be destroyed by his will or by the bishop's love: a self-love so overpowering that this loftiest soul — unwilling to allow Fauchelevent to die in order to avert Javert's suspicions, unafraid to incite in Javert the desire for vengeance that leads him to denounce the mayor to the police after Madeleine overrides the prison sentence imposed by the inspector on Fantine — is now prepared to perpetrate the gravest evil for the sake of his self-perpetuation. To protect himself from being exposed as a thief he is prepared to become "the most odious of thieves ... robbing a man of his life, his peace, his place in the sun, morally murdering him by condemning him to the living death that is called a convict prison." [D214] In his previous tests — whether or not to lift the cart, whether or not to antagonize Javert over Fantine — love has won out. But in all previous situations the risk of personal destruction was just that, a risk. Now Madeleine no longer *risks* anything; that he will bring about his own destruction by saving the other man is a sure thing. Yet only in being coerced by his will-to-live to let another man rot is Madeleine forced to see the promise to the bishop stripped to its final implication: if the promise to become an honest man means — as Jean Valjean had decided — the command to love the other as oneself, then, in a situation where the self cannot stay afloat without drowning the other, the command to love finds its own final meaning in the most beautifully terrible words in existence: "Greater love hath no man than this, that a man lay down his life for his friends." (John 15:13)

These words, whose binding power Madeleine cannot disavow, bisect his ineradicable desire to lay down the life of the falsely arrested Valjean so that Madeleine can continue to be. In this way is he nailed to the cross formed by the intersection of the drive for self-preservation — sometimes frenzied, usually covert — that propels us forward one minute after the next and makes self-love inevitable, and the Law of Love that cuts against egotism at every instant but usually remains under anesthesia so long as circumstance does not tear through the luxury of keeping it numbed. It is this cross that turns his hair white. At the moment Madeleine reaches the initial decision to let the other man go to prison in his place, this cross is erected in the form of a single question he unwillingly finds in his mind: "Had he not had a greater purpose, the saving not of his life but of his soul?" [D214] This is Hugo's bare-boned version of Luke 9: 23-26: "If anyone would come after me, let him deny himself and take up his cross daily and follow me. For whoever would save his life will lose it, but whoever loses his life for my sake will save it. For what does it profit a man if he gains the whole world and loses or forfeits himself?"

The parallels of *Les Misérables* with the biblical text are obvious. Hugo describes Madeleine as hounded by "that mysterious power which said to him, 'Reflect,' as two thousand years before it had said to another condemned man, 'Take up thy Cross!'" [D213] To save himself, "to do nothing, was in fact to do *everything*: it was to descend to the most abject depths of criminal hypocrisy and cowardice." [D214]

> But if, on the other hand, he saved the man by repairing the blunder, by proclaiming himself Jean Valjean the felon, this would be to achieve his own true resurrection and firmly close the door on the hell from which he firmly sought to escape. To return to it in appearance would be to escape from it in reality. This is what he must do, and without it he would have accomplished nothing, his life would be wasted, his repentance meaningless, and there would be nothing left for him to say except, 'Who cares?' He felt the presence of the bishop, more urgent than in life; he felt the old bishop's eyes upon him and knew that henceforth Madeleine the mayor, with all his virtues, would seem to him abominable, whereas Jean Valjean the felon would be admirable and pure. Other men would see the mask, but the bishop would see the face; others would see the life, but he would see the soul. So there was nothing for it but to go to Arras and rescue the false Jean Valjean by proclaiming the true one. The most heartrending of sacrifices, the most poignant of victories, the ultimate, irretrievable step — but it had to be done. It was his most melancholy destiny that he could achieve sanctity in the eyes of God only by returning to degradation in the eyes of men. [D214]

*The second cross of Monsieur Madeleine:*
*Conclusion #3: Fantine, the town, need me*

It is to Hugo's credit as an artist that this powerful resolution — Madeleine is said to have spat out in disgust
his initial decision to do nothing — likewise does not
hold. The force with which the Law of Love cuts against
the will to self-preservation is soon cut against with equal
force by the strength of Madeleine's desire not to be Jean
Valjean. Reinhold Niebuhr defines tragedy as

> conscious choices of evil for the sake of good. If
> men or nations do evil in a good cause; if they
> cover themselves with guilt in order to fulfill some
> high responsibility; or if they sacrifice some high
> value for the sake of a higher or equal one they
> make a tragic choice.[1]

Madeleine is faced with a classic tragic choice between two high values — the life of a man who does
enormous good (himself), and the life of another. He
has reversed his first conclusion to remain as Madeleine
because it concealed hypocrisy: his own goodness — not
to be doubted — was a pretext; the choice he was *really*
making was to destroy another man to protect himself.
Hence, his second conclusion: that he must confess to
being Jean Valjean. Against this, he now constructs a
new line of defense, subtler than the first, born when he
unexpectedly remembers Fantine. "I've been thinking
only of myself!" he argues. "I've only considered what
suits me! It suits me either to keep quiet or to give myself

---

[1] Reinhold Niebuhr, *The Irony of American History* (New
York: Charles Scribner's and Sons, 1952), vii.

up, to hide myself or to save my soul, to be a magistrate, despicable but respected, or a galley slave, disgraced but noble, it's all about me, me, me, me, nothing but me! ... Talk about sheer egotism! Different forms of egotism, but egotism just the same! How about thinking of others for a change? The first sacred duty is to think of one's neighbor." [R193]

Fantine, he continues, needs him! In fact, she dies the instant she is aware he no longer has the power to help her. Without him, Fantine's little daughter Cosette will be thrown out into the streets and is likely to die. Moreover, the town needs him! In fact, after his disappearance the townspeople devour one another with greed and all that was built up is destroyed. Thus even truth is used to sustain the lie as he reverts to the first decision. "My mind is made up. I shall leave things as they are and there will be no more vacillation. I am Madeleine and will continue to be Madeleine, and as for the man who now bears the name of Valjean, so much the worse for him." [D218]

He removes from a concealed cupboard his prison garb, the stick with which he frightened the child Petit-Gervais and the coin he stole from him. He throws them into the fire to burn all condemning traces of his past. He begins to burn the candlesticks, the first already stirring the coals when an inner voice cries out: "Destroy the candlesticks ... forget the bishop ... You will enrich the town, feed the poor, protect the orphan and live happy in the light of every man's esteem while another man wears the blue smock and fetters that are rightly yours ... How fortunately things have turned out for you." [D219]

### *Decision impossible; indecision impossible*

So Madeleine again falters, no closer to a decision at dawn than when Javert walked out the door the previous afternoon. "Whichever way he turned he faced the same alternatives — to cling to his paradise and become a devil, or become a saint by going back to hell." [D221] He had seen the arrest of the luckless stranger headed for prison in his place as a God-given destiny so that he, Madeleine, could continue his benevolence. And he had seen the arrest of the luckless stranger headed for prison in his place as a God-given destiny so that he, Jean Valjean, would plunge into hell, simultaneously redeeming and ruining himself by saving the arrested man. In truth, his real destiny is: to CHOOSE! But to choose is a paradox. The promise to the bishop contains as one of its most fundamental elements the freedom not to be bound by the promise. However overpowering the will to preserve himself, he is free not to be bound by that drive. Nothing forces him to allow a man to be destroyed through his silence. The self-centeredness that corrupts the heart at every moment has not the power to corrupt it at any particular moment. There is nothing in human nature or human destiny that can finally block any ego from saying "NO" to its egotism at any moment in time, even at the cost of one's life.

### *The cross as ambivalence*

Yet, at no point as he moves toward the courthouse can Madeleine erase his ambivalence, just as he never shakes his ambivalence toward Marius until the final pages of the novel. Ambivalence belongs to the cross, as the cross belongs to the structure of honest selfhood, even for an atheist such as myself. Still, when the carriage he has hired the previous day arrives before dawn with Madeleine still undecided, he grabs hold of the reins. Hugo writes that he was driving blindly, not knowing where, through the darkness and into an abyss. Yet he heads toward Arras where the trial is to be held. He tells himself it is merely to observe the proceedings at first hand, or to confirm the worthlessness of the arrested man in order to ease his conscience about letting him take the fall; nonetheless he moves forward. The wheel of the carriage breaks; he is relentless in his attempts to have it repaired, to hire another carriage — or at least, a horse — and when all efforts fail, is ecstatic with relief. Telling himself he has tried his best and earned the right to turn back, an old woman appears with an offer of a carriage. He recoils, then investigates. Warned it is a wreck, he takes it anyway, angry that he had rejoiced in the failure to proceed. The boy who had brought his need for the cart to the attention of the old woman asks for a tip; the always overgenerous Madeleine rudely whips his horse to get away from the "nauseating" request and moves on — to Arras.

The courthouse is full when he arrives, no room for even one more person says the court usher guarding the closed door. Except, the usher adds after a pause, for one or two seats behind the presiding judge's chair for those holding public office. Madeleine departs, only to return with a note in his hand introducing himself as the mayor. The judge is brought the note and gives the ok; the mayor is left alone in the judges' chamber behind the courtroom and need simply open the door. His eyes fall on the brass door handle. Sweat starts to roll down his temples and with the words: "Who says I must?" he flees again down a series of passageways and stairs, stops dead in his tracks shivering, then once more reverses himself. Returning to the judges' chamber, the door handle to the courtroom leaps out at him. He moves toward it in fits-and-starts until without knowing how it happened he is standing at the closed door, no less split than when his ordeal began.

If love is simply emotion, what could have brought him to the court? No human being can feel sufficient emotion to destroy himself for someone he has never seen. If love is will, as is sometimes said to those who wish to break earlier promises when the emotion we call love dies, then it is a superfluous word and can be re-named duty. What exactly does it mean to "Take up thy Cross?" A strange demand, especially for one like myself, with no connection to the Christian salvation. Yet I am convinced this cross exists independently of Christianity and every other religion, that in its reality alone is to be explained the question posed at the outset of why a generation notorious for self-absorption could be so existentially affected by a drama of self-sacrifice. Somerset Maugham writes in *The Razor's Edge*: "Self-sacrifice is a passion so powerful that beside it even lust and hunger pale by comparison. It whirls its victim to destruction in the highest affirmation of his personality."[1] No one who has ever been touched by Jean Valjean could easily sneak past the profundity of these words. Every tear shed on his account confirms that the highest form of self is self-lessness, that in his willingness, despite his ambivalence,

---

[1] Somerset Maugham, *The Razor's Edge* (New York: Vintage International, 2003), 208.

to crush himself, he affirms not only his highest humanity but holds us to account before our own. The lure of his beauty is equaled only by the dread of imitating his austere road.

With a convulsive movement, Madeleine opens the courtroom door. Only one thing differs from the room in which he was tried twenty-seven years earlier. On the wall, above the head of the presiding judge: a crucifix.

*Part Three*

# JAVERT VERSUS VALJEAN

A thousand pages into the story, having been ruth-lessly hunted by Javert for years, the escaped convict Jean Valjean is offered the possibility of executing him. Valjean cuts the ropes that bind him and lets him go. Javert makes an astounding response. "I'd rather you killed me." [D1040]

*Why* would he rather be killed than saved?

Hugo says of him: "The Asturian peasants believe that in every wolf-litter there is a dog-whelp which the mother kills, because otherwise when it grows larger it will devour the rest of her young. Endow this dog with a human face, and you have Javert." [D165] The image evokes criminality and, ironically, Javert was born in prison. But if there is a component of criminality in Javert it is in pursuit of a good — for him the absolute and final good: Justice. Justice, which for Javert means the holy trinity of Justice-Authority-Law, is an object of religious worship. "He was a spy in the way that other men are priests." [D166]

"Composite ... monk and army corporal, that spy in-capable of falsehood," [D194] Javert is an unflinching ascetic, living for his justice-god a life of austerity, isolation, self-denial, and chastity. Indeed it is striking that of the four characters marked by greatness in the story — the bishop, Jean Valjean, Javert, and the revolutionary leader Enjolras — all are celibate, and all except the bishop, who was married and amorous in his youth, virgins. I

41

wonder if even Hugo was aware of this. The strange fact remains that Javert shares many of the ascetic qualities of his nemesis Jean Valjean: renunciation of pleasure and friendship, a strong bent for solitude, complete absence of vice (a pinch of snuff when pleased with himself is "his sole concession to human frailty" [D167]), vast resources of inner calm, even a longing for transcendence of the state of man. In the service of "the police force [that] had been his true religion," "Javert's ideal was to be more than human." [D1106]

He is a man of principle and, as an absolutist, must devote himself to the *highest* principle. All else has value only so long as it serves this highest; what does not serve justice is to Javert a matter of indifference, incomprehension or — far worse: the object of his wrath if it obstructs his cause. This explains his response to love. When Madeleine lifts the cart to save Fauchelevent, Javert is astounded by his strength. But the beauty of the gesture — beautiful above all because both men know that if the mayor lifts the cart he may be tipping off the already suspicious inspector as to his real identity — leaves Javert utterly unmoved. Nor does Madeleine's sacrifice mean anything to the Inspector of Police in human terms, or in any way mitigate the fact that if the mayor *is* Jean Valjean, he must be struck down by the full force of the law. The love that abolished Fantine's prison sentence, by contrast, simply gets in his way. It is "a false indulgence which undermines society," [D200] and makes of the mayor an enemy of both society and its guardian, Inspector Javert.

## A cop and a mayor volley over Fantine

As the quarrel over Fantine marks the first overt battle between Javert and Jean Valjean, it is worth recalling the event. The once beautiful woman is, at 26, shriveled, tubercular and decrepit. One of four women abandoned simultaneously by their lovers as a joke, Fantine had been left to raise her equally abandoned child. If exposed as the mother of a bastard she cannot work. So bowing to realities with the heaviest of hearts, with no idea of what she is letting herself and the child in for, she arranges for the vile Thénardiers to raise her daughter Cosette for a monthly fee. These foster-parents keep upping the price for the child they torment and hate, and when Fantine is discovered to have given birth out of wedlock she is — unbeknownst to Mayor Madeleine — dismissed from his factory and made destitute, in due course selling her gorgeous blond hair, then her front teeth. Ceaseless demands by the Thénardiers for repayment of fabricated medical expenses force Fantine to "sell the rest." When a dandy at a cafe abuses the now repulsive whore with sarcasms, her disinterest rouses him to throw snow down the back of the sick woman's low-cut gown (destroying her weakened health). Fantine strikes back in fury, is arrested by Javert, and sentenced to a prison term of six months.

The mayor, stumbling upon the scene and learning through inquiries it was the dandy who was the aggressor, immediately heads to the police station. Fantine is pleading for mercy as he arrives. Javert responds: "You're getting six months, and the Eternal Father himself can't alter it." Madeleine intervenes; Fantine (blaming him for her lost job and downfall) spits in his face. Madeleine responds: "Inspector Javert, this woman is to go free," flabbergasting Fantine. Javert counters that this cannot be allowed; moreover, she has spat at the mayor. Madeleine says: "That is my affair." Javert denies this: "Forgive me, Monsieur le maire, the insult was not to yourself but to justice." Madeleine, observing that the case belongs to the municipal rather than the state police, overrides him: "You must be quite clear about this. She will not serve a single day in prison."D185-9 The astounded Fantine glances rapidly from one to the other as they battle out whether Madeleine's love or Javert's justice is to determine her fate. Finally, the mayor pulls rank and orders her release, putting himself in triple jeopardy in the eyes of Javert: for violating the principle of justice as such; for being unjust to Javert in particular by denying him his right to carry out his duty; by festering in consequence within Javert the most dubious form of justice — revenge — which, however abhorrent, still can be an expression of justice. This, congealing with his earlier suspicions, prompts Javert to denounce the mayor as Jean Valjean, convict number 24601, in a letter to the Paris police.

The event marks the second time love and justice square off in *Les Misérables*. In one sense it is a recapitulation of the encounter between Jean Valjean and the bishop. Fantine has fallen as Valjean had fallen. Justice claims the right to punishment. But love intervenes to override those claims. Deceived by the lie of the bishop, however, the police were not aware that justice *had* any claims. Javert by contrast, embodies those claims; exactly this is his vocation, and for love to intervene is for him an injustice that cannot be tolerated.

## When justice is superior to forgiveness

It is hard not to cringe at the injustice of Javert's "justice." Yet he represents a counterforce to the idea that society can be run on the basis of the love of the Sermon on the Mount. Years earlier the bishop remarks to the dying revolutionary G: "The judge speaks in the name of justice. The priest speaks in the name of pity, which is only a higher form of justice." [D53] Javert had he been there would have told the bishop — and would not have been wrong: a society that replaces justice with loving pity would be destroyed, and if it survived it would be unjust. Abuse consistently forgiven means tyranny; imagine Nazi Germany forgiven without having first broken its power. So in one sense he is correct in resisting the mayor, who tells Javert in the fight over Fantine: "Conscience is the highest justice." [D188] The conscience of the bishop would invariably think it just to turn the other cheek, sweeping the Thénardiers of this world to power. Javert, "the destroying angel," [D267] will endure every hardship to ensure that they do not, which is why Hugo consistently emphasizes his greatness, though, he remarks, it is greatness in perversion.

## The evil in good

Nowhere is this perversion clearer than in Javert's frenzied joy at the destruction of Monsieur Madeleine. For six weeks following their quarrel over Fantine at police headquarters the Inspector avoids him. Suddenly, Javert appears in Madeleine's office to demand—of all things— his own dismissal! His letter denouncing the mayor to the Prefecture of Police in Paris, he confesses, was an injustice against authority. Javert is certain of this because the "real" Jean Valjean has been arrested. Resignation from his post, an honorable proceeding, must not be allowed him. Javert insists he must be fired. His next words reveal the essence of his character. "Monsieur le maire, you treated me unjustly not long ago [over Fantine]. This time you must deal with me justly." D195

Madeleine's merciful response — insisting Javert has exaggerated his offense, that he deserves to rise in the world not plummet, that he remain on the job, offering the inspector his hand as they part — is unacceptable to Javert, whose final reasoning says all. He has, he tells the mayor, been harsh with others in his life, and justly so. If he were not equally harsh with himself now, "all my past acts would be unjustified." Javert continues: "It would be abominable and the people who talk about 'that swine Javert' would be right. I do not wish for your indulgence, Monsieur le maire, I have been exasperated enough by your indulgence for others ... God knows, it's easy to be kind; the hard thing is to be just. If you had turned out to be what I suspected, Monsieur le maire, I should have shown you no kindness! ... It is right that I be dismissed and broken." D200

So departs this "strangely honest man with a bizarre greatness" D201 and, as always, he has not lied, for when at Fantine's bedside to arrest Madeleine the day after the mayor goes to the court to denounce himself, Javert is as distant from kindness and mercy as it is humanly possible to be. The "face of the fiend," Hugo writes of him, hideous in his jubilation that it is the scoundrel Madeleine, not Javert, who is to be broken: "upright, arrogant and resplendent," the "mailed fist of the absolute," "the embodiment ... of the superhuman ferocity of the destroying angel," "the personification of justice, light and truth in their sublime task of stamping out evil." [D267]

> Yet in this outrageous St. Michael there was a greatness that could not be gainsaid. He was terrible, but he was not ignoble. Integrity, sincerity, honesty, conviction, the sense of duty, these are qualities which, being misguided, may become hideous, but they still retain their greatness; amid the hideousness, the nobility proper to human conscience still persists. They are virtues subject to a single vice, that of error. The merciless but honest rejoicing of a fanatic performing an atrocious act still has a melancholy claim to our respect. Without knowing it, Javert in his awful happiness was deserving of pity, like every ignorant man who triumphs. Nothing could have been more poignant or more heartrending than that countenance on which was inscribed all the evil in what is good. [D267-8]

### Javert calm

Why, then, would Javert, for whom the destruction of Valjean was "a mystical obsession," [D268] eight years later, at the brink of death, rather be killed by Valjean than set free?

Behind the barricade built by the anti-monarchist republicans in the 1832 attempt to ignite the people to overthrow the state, Javert, undercover, is unmasked by the child-revolutionary Gavroche (who viewers of the musical would not realize is Thénardier's neglected son). "Who are you?" Enjolras, the leader of the insurrection, demands of the accused. Javert responds with "the most disdainful, unabashed, and resolute of smiles." Asked if he is a police informer, "that spy incapable of falsehood" identifies himself as "a representative of the law," freely giving his name. He is tied hand and foot and secured to a post in the tavern that serves as insurrection headquarters, completely silent at his sudden reversal of fate and confronts his captors "with the cool serenity of a man who has never in his life told a lie." [D937-8] The following day as he is once more tied to a table with a bayonet against his chest, Jean Valjean — come to the barricade to save Marius — appears in the tavern doorway. Javert, with the same calm, utters his first words to Valjean since 1823: "So here we are!" [D1008]

What could account for his serenity when their last encounter left Javert in exasperated rage? The source of that rage had been this: during the first weeks in Paris after the rescue of Cosette from the Thénardiers, a beggar huddled nightly under a street lamp gets accustomed to receiving alms from Jean Valjean; one night as his benefactor places a coin in his hand, the beggar looks up and Jean Valjean is shocked in the dim light by "a tiger in the dark," [D396] the face of a different man — Javert! The beggar, a police informant, is back at his post the next evening but the damage is done: a few nights later Javert has Valjean cornered, little Cosette in his arms, in a cul-de-sac of Paris. Only through the impossible assent of a steep wall does Jean Valjean, "with the aspirations of a saint … with the formidable talents of a criminal," [D407] elude capture. The convent he thus providentially enters earns him and Cosette five years of sanctuary, and earns Javert, "one of the most shrewd and able detectives that ever lived," [D424] years of remorse for a rare strategic blunder: he had postponed Valjean's capture for "the childish satisfaction of toying with a man of that calibre" [D424] when he had him in his sights.

### Valjean's revenge

Now, these many years later, with the barricade close to falling and the revolutionaries aware that they are doomed, Enjolras puts a pistol on the table and orders the last man alive to "blow out this spy's brains" at a spot just outside the barricade. "We don't want his body to be mixed up with our own." [D1037-8] As always, Enjolras is tranquil. "Only one man at that moment was more impassive than Enjolras; it was Javert himself." [D1038] Valjean asks to be allowed to perform the execution. Grateful to him for having earlier saved the barricade from destruction, he is given the task as a reward. Valjean takes hold of his pursuer. Javert laughs and coolly says to the soon to be killed insurrectionists: "You're hardly any better off than I am." [R1010]

The men rush from the tavern to resist the final assault on the barricade, leaving Valjean and Javert alone. Valjean unties the rope that binds his captive to the table and commands him, hands and feet still tied — to stand. Javert obeys, writes Hugo, "with the indefinable smile which is the expression of captive supremacy" — the smile possible only for those able to live by the line of Seneca: "He who can die cannot be coerced." This is the meaning of the "profound calm" with which, glimpsing the dead Eponine among the pile of corpses, Javert utters his first humane words in the novel: "I think I know that girl."

49

"Take your revenge," he says to Jean Valjean. Valjean stuffs the pistol under his arm and pulls out a knife. "A knife thrust! You're quite right. That suits you better," adds Javert, the knife proving Valjean is the low-life the Inspector assessed him as all along. Valjean's response is to cut the ropes binding Javert's wrists and ankles. "You're free to go," he says. Javert's mouth drops in shock. Valjean adds that in the unlikely event he does not die in the barricade, Javert can find him at number 7, Rue de l' Homme-Armé. Javert, tigerish, warns Valjean to beware. "Off you go," Valjean tells him. [R1011] With summoned dignity Javert walks off but after a few paces turns back before departing; it is then that he says: "I find this embarrassing. I'd rather you killed me." This concludes the chapter entitled "The Vengeance of Jean Valjean."[D1039-40]

Javert could die with "utmost composure" in the service of justice — through his attempt to bring the enemies of the state to heel. Even on the personal level he admits Jean Valjean's right to revenge, the lowest form of justice from the lowest form of man. His "smile of captive supremacy" is his final mockery, a farewell assertion of vast moral superiority over the insurrectionists, above all the vermin Jean Valjean. The vermin lets Javert go.

*Javert dazed*

When the two next meet, Jean Valjean, caked in excrement, has just emerged from the sewer with the dying Marius on his back. Javert does not recognize him; only when Valjean identifies himself does Javert seize him — his gaze terrible, their faces almost touching — and stare wildly into his face. He seems not to hear Valjean say he has no intention of escaping but would like, before his arrest, to return Marius to his grandfather. When, releasing his grip, Javert finally asks —"What are you doing here? Who is this man?" — he speaks "as though in a dream." [D1096] His state of shock parallels Valjean's in the aftermath of his encounter with the bishop. "His feelings," Hugo writes of his confusion, were "partly those of a wolf catching its prey and partly those of a dog finding its master." [D1104]

Arrested by Javert at dying Fantine's bedside ten years before, Valjean had begged for three days to retrieve her child. Javert contemptuously refused. *This* time the cop calls for a carriage and in preoccupied silence accompanies Valjean and what he thinks is Marius's corpse to the grandfather's home. The deed completed, he seizes Valjean by the arm and leads him again into the carriage. Valjean's request for one final favor — to stop at home for a moment en route to prison — is harshly met. Yet Javert breaks his silence by calling out to the driver Valjean's address. Upon arrival the Inspector pays the fare and sends the carriage away. Informing Valjean he'll wait for him outside "it cost him an effort to speak." [D1099] Valjean assumes they will proceed on foot to the nearest police post once he has wakened Cosette, told her Marius is alive, and made any last hurried arrangements. Climbing the stairs to her room he looks out onto the street from an open window. Javert is gone.

### Valjean's challenge to Javert

Valjean's sparing of Javert's life is an unjust act of loving mercy. An act which deprives Javert of the dignity of a just death, but it is much more. The will to self-preservation is as strong in Javert as in any man. However prepared to die, he cannot help being grateful to be alive, which means being grateful to love. Javert could have easily gone back into the barricade if a just death was all that he wanted; at first sight one of the insurgents would have gladly gunned him down. Instead, he accepts Jean Valjean's gift. From that decision on, every future breath is on the basis of another man's mercy.

That the giver of this mercy is someone Javert would have brought down in ecstasy had the situation been reversed is a spiritual catastrophe as decisive as was Valjean's after the forgiving lie of the bishop. How can it be that this person he has hunted *without mercy* for so long has let him go? If he cannot deny Jean Valjean's love towards him — and he cannot deny it without denying his undeniable relief at not having died — then he cannot deny the love that drove the convict-mayor to rescue his falsely arrested look-alike, to save Fauchelevent from the cart, to save Fantine from prison, to save Cosette from the Thénardiers, and now to save Marius. "Behind Valjean loomed the figure of Monsieur Madeleine, and they merged into one, into a figure deserving of veneration." D1106

For Javert, this cannot be.

His "I'd rather you killed me" means, in its interrogative form: "Why did you let me go? *Who* are you, Valjean? What does an existence such as yours mean?" Valjean's answer lies not only in cutting Javert's ropes, but in telling him his address. The cutting of the rope declares: *I am love.* Javert might have opposed that with: "And I am justice, which is superior!" The giving of his address says: *If justice is truly greater than love, you must arrest me.*

52

*Javert and Valjean twins — but not identical*

Javert wants to re-arrest him, needs to re-arrest him — for the same reason Jean Valjean had once wanted to drive a spike into the skull of the bishop: to deny love's supremacy. He cannot arrest him, in the words of Richard DeMartino, "because Javert realizes that Jean Valjean is ten thousand times greater than him as a human being." Valjean's life was transformed by committing an action of which he was no longer capable: the theft of a child's coin. Javert too must commit an act of which he is no longer capable. His inability to do so at once elevates him and destroys him.

He may have been able to survive on the basis of Jean Valjean's love; what undoes him is that Javert's response is to act so that the man to whom he owes his life, owes his life to him. "He was amazed that Valjean should have shown him mercy, and that he should have shown Valjean mercy in return." [D1105]

His entire career he was without qualm — in justice's name — in destroying the perpetrators of loving acts that violated the law. Even after letting Jean Valjean go "he did not for a moment deny that the law was the law."[D1106] "Only one proper course lay open to him — to hurry back to the Rue de l'Homme-Armé and seize Valjean. He knew it well, but he could not do it." [D1105]

Javert struggles mightily in the last hour of his life to withstand Valjean's onslaught. "Try as he might, he had in his heart to admit the scoundrel's greatness." [D1106] He sets against this greatness the full majesty of the law. But at his determination to enforce the law "in the back of his mind a voice, a strange voice, cried out to him: 'Go on, then. Hand over your savior. Then have them bring you Pontius Pilate's washbasin and wash your claws.'"[R1082]

It is striking how intent Hugo is — in the section "Javert in Disarray" that records the Inspector's suicide — to drive home the cost of Javert's mercy. "Something new, a revolution, a disaster, had occurred to him." [D1104] "He had been torn up by the roots. The code he lived by was in fragments in his hand." "The whole structure of his life collapsed." [D1106] "All the principles on which his estimate of man had been based were overthrown." [D1105] "He felt that his life was in ruins. Authority was dead within him, and he had no reason to go on living." [D1107]

*Javert, the merciful, killed by love*

When Javert first appears in the novel Hugo says of him, highlighting his fanaticism and rejection of moral ambiguity: "He drew a straight line through all that is most tortuous in the world." [D166] Now, he writes: "What was happening to Javert resembled the de-railing of a train — the straight line of the soul broken by the presence of God. God, the inwardness of man, the true conscience as opposed to the false, the eternal splendid presence." [D1107] Just as the bishop cuts vertically against Valjean — as the demand to be selfless with which Jean must ever after collide — so is Javert derailed by the bisecting cut of Valjean, thereby forming the cross that nails from then on all his forward existence.

But the result is not the same. Hugo writes of Javert: "He was not so much transformed as a victim of this miracle." He is now "forced to admit ... that judges are men and even the law may do wrong." [D1107] Forced to admit that his justice has been a foul abstract legalism incapable of bending to the concrete situation, hence blinding himself to the fact that sending Fantine to prison was an outrage while crushing Thénardier was not. Forced to admit — in being compelled to let Valjean go, in being unable to re-arrest him having let him go — that there are "cases when the law, mumbling excuses, must bow to transfigured crime," [D1107] and that what Mayor Madeleine had told him in nullifying Fantine's prison sentence is *sometimes* true: "Conscience is the highest justice." [D188] "He could no longer live by his lifelong principles; he had entered a new strange world of humanity, mercy, gratitude and justice other than that of the law." [D1106] But he had entered that world by force, by the inability to do otherwise. He had received mercy, had responded with mercy, but Javert is deformed, not transformed. He "submitted [to the miracle of receiving and bestowing mercy] in exasperation, feeling that henceforth his very breath must fail." [D1107]

And so, after composing a final report to the Prefecture of Police in which he stiffly requests remedies to a list of minor police injustices that victimize convicts serving time, Javert kills himself. His suicide is his last act of justice, punishment against himself for having violated the law in letting a convict go free. It is also the consequence of Javert, an obsessive absolutist, having lost a standpoint on which to live. Javert can no longer accept — because despite himself he has not in the most critical action of his life accepted — the law as the foundation of righteous existence. Nor can he base his life in justice. For justice, to his shock, can attain the truth that Javert must live by only if it is rooted in a higher principle: love. Javert cannot love. He does not *want* to love. In the rubble of inner earthquake the most he could retrieve "under the granite ... [was] something contradictory that is almost a heart." [D1107] His suicide is his answer to the dilemma that "so overwhelmed him." [D1105] "There were only two ways out. To go determinedly to Jean Valjean and return him to prison, or else ... " [D1108]

Derailed by and into the presence of God, Javert knows that he cannot obey. But Javert's code is that a superior must be obeyed, "that, faced by a superior with whom he does not agree, he can only resign. But how resign from God?" [D1107]

All that is left him is the single act that makes the divine presence and divine forgiveness impossible. Yet Javert had years before said he had no right to resign. "To resign is an honorable proceeding," he had told the Mayor Madeleine. "I have committed an offense and I must be punished for it. I must be dismissed." [D195]

It comes to a plunge in the Seine either way. A resignation: a last act of justice against himself through which he also does justice *to* himself in a final affirmation of the principle to which he had dedicated his life. A dismissal: a just sentence for one who had betrayed both his principle and his life at the crucial moment.

And this combined with another contradiction entirely: the final act of a man who realizes he must love and can't, who must not be merciful and was, and who now sees in the river a Void that wills him, in his last words in the musical: "To escape the world of Jean Valjean."

*Part Four*

# CROSS —

# OR DOUBLE CROSS

There is a Zen saying: "He's won the hat on his head but lost the sandals from his feet." Jean Valjean, spiritual Hercules who "had been almost a villain and had become almost a saint,"[D770] in successive battles between love and self-love defied Javert's suspicion and lifted the cart off the dying Fauchelevent; chose to go back to prison for the rest of his life in order to save a falsely arrested innocent from the same horrible fate; ignited in the Thénardiers, both husband and wife, a life-long desire for vengeance by taking Cosette from their clutches at too cheap a price. Eight years later, held hostage by Thénardier and his gang, Valjean responds to their demand for Cosette's address ( — they plan to take her hostage as well until Valjean pays out an enormous ransom —) with a majestic: "My own life is not much worth defending. As for making me talk — or making me write anything I don't want to write, or say anything I don't want to say ... Well, look!" [D694] He seizes a burning-hot chisel from the fire and sears it into his bare forearm. Even his hardened captors gasp.

He can die for his daughter without flinching. What he *cannot* do average men accomplish daily the world over: let a daughter grow up, fall in love, marry, and separate from her dad. That this is the cross that thwarts him — that after so many spiritual victories where the stakes were life-and-death a common domestic matter topples him at a time of safety when Javert is not even on his trail — here is the greatness of Victor Hugo as a psychologist.

The first red flag is in the convent, where Jean Valjean hides from the police as a gardener's assistant for five years. He achieves "peace and silence and simplicity" there. "His whole heart was melted in gratitude, and his love was magnified." [D491] Among the causes of this blessed serenity are the nuns, the cloister, the love he and Cosette bestow on one another — and, scarily — those "moments when it pleased him to think that she would never be pretty." [D394]

"She was his and ... nothing could take her from him, ... certainly she would become a nun." [D758] They would remain in the convent until he was dead and she grew old. But this "ecstatic thought" made Valjean uneasy. Would his happiness "not be gained at the expense of another person, a child, whereas he was already an old man; ... in short, ... was [it] not an act of theft?" What if she later regretted that a nun's life had been imposed on her? He feared "Cosette would come to hate him." It is this last thought — "almost a selfish one" — that leads Valjean to conclude "the child had a right to know something about the world before renouncing it." [D758] So they set up house — three houses, precisely, due to his ingrained fear of the police — Valjean 60, Cosette 14. When he takes her about Paris, Cosette happily clinging to his arm with an "affection which she reserved so exclusively for himself," the rapturous Valjean "told himself, poor man, that this is a state of affairs that would last as long as he lived." [D769]

That by sixteen Cosette becomes a radiant beauty instills in him "a sense of profound, indefinable unease." "The glow which enveloped her represented a threat in his possessive eyes."[D770] At the incursion of Marius even into the periphery of her life "he trembled in the depths of his mind" and "took a hearty dislike" to him.[D775-6] "He darted fierce and threatening glances at the young man. He who had thought himself no longer capable of any malice now felt the return of an old, wild savagery."[D777]

Years ago I heard this from a friend: her nephew, in a school election for class president, "negated" himself by voting for the other candidate. His opponent voted for himself. The nephew, losing the election by one vote, felt betrayed. He had "lost himself to gain himself," thinking that gain meant a reward. It's a simple story but helps explain Valjean's expectation of a payback for his saintly life:

> After living for sixty years on my knees, suffering everything that can be suffered, growing old without having ever been young, living without a family, without wife or children or friends; after leaving my blood on every stone and every thorn, ... after returning good for evil and kindness for cruelty; after making myself an honest man in spite of everything, repenting of my sins and forgiving those who have sinned against me — after all this, when at last I have received my reward, when I have got what I want and know that it is good and that I have deserved it — now it is to be snatched from me! I am to lose Cosette and with her my whole life, all the happiness I have ever had, simply be-

cause a young oaf chooses to come idling in the Luxembourg! [D777]

*If the cross is so great, why not double it?*

What Victor Hugo calls Thénardier's "gamble with life" [D635] amounts to this twist on the Gospel: if you try to save yourself you *may, possibly*, lose yourself, but if you lose yourself for anyone's sake you're an idiot. If self-negation is Valjean's path to salvation, other-negation is Thénardier's. "Egotism, Monsieur le Baron, is the law of life ... Everyone for himself. Self-interest is the object of all men and money is the loadstone." [D1182] These are Thénardier's remarks to Marius at the end of the novel as he fails to sell him the secret of his father-in-law Jean Valjean's identity for 20,000 francs, fails again for 10,000, then, with his inveterate adaptability suggests: "But I've got to eat haven't I? ... I will let you have it for 20 francs." [D1184] Thénardier is the possibility that the gospel teaching in Mark 9:35 — "If anyone would be first, he must be last of all and servant of all" — is a lie. He is the external embodiment of that element within Jean Valjean that wants to step down from the cross and live a life of "me first." Through the bishop, through his own inner struggles, later in the convent, Valjean came to know that "the sublime height of self-abnegation ... [is] the highest possible peak of virtue." [D490] Now, desperate at the prospect of losing Cosette to Marius, he repents ever leaving the convent — "that Paradise from which he had voluntarily exiled himself" — for the exact opposite reason: "he now regretted the mood of self-abnegation and folly which had prompted him to bring Cosette out into the world." [D778]

That's Thénardier talking within him. It is crucial to the novel that with but nine pages left, Thénardier is more certain of victory by his standards than Valjean — who has negated himself into a forlorn illness and death by lovingly separating himself from Cosette — is by his. For Thénardier has at long last hit the jackpot: Marius, undeceived by the scoundrel, has thrown four thousand francs at him and guaranteed a letter of credit for another twenty thousand. The "incurable" Thénardier gobbles up the money and within forty-eight hours emigrates with his wife and remaining daughter to America — where he invests in the slave trade! The fact is that Thénardier is never defeated by his defeats. He is the playing out, over the decades of the book, of a question that until the final scenes Valjean can never entirely erase from his mind: Isn't the bishop, with his unspoken injunction that self-lessness trump egoism, sometimes wrong?

### Thénardier: "puny despot" and man of the stage

Hugo writes: "There are human creatures which, like crayfish, always retreat into shadow, going backwards rather than forwards through life, gaining in deformity with experience, going from bad to worse and sinking into even deeper darkness. The Thénardiers were of this kind."[D150-1] Both, we are told, "were dwarfish natures ... highly susceptible to the encroachments of evil." [D150] The husband is described as "a Jack-of-all-trades who did everything badly." [D151] This applies to his literary pretensions as well as his attempts at a crime whose payoff will be, as Thénardier puts it: "to be able to eat my fill and drink my fill, guzzle to my heart's content and sleep it off,

63

and never a stroke of work ... Before I die I want to know what it feels like to live like a millionaire." D658

William Hazlett's comment on Shakespeare's Iago — "He is an amateur of tragedy in real life; and, instead of employing his invention on imaginary characters or long-forgotten incidents, he takes the bolder and more dangerous course of getting up his plot at home, casts the principal parts among his nearest friends and connections, and rehearses it in down-right earnest, with steady nerves and unabated resolution" (Bradley 1991:215) — would apply to Thénardier, if his plays weren't such flops. It's no accident that of the four forged letters begging for handouts that Marius finds in the packet dropped by the Thénardier daughters, one is signed: "P. Fabentou, artist of the drama," and a second by an aspiring dramatist: "Genflot, man of letters." But Hugo does not mean the theater when he records Thénardier's own judgment that "no stage worthy of his considerable talents had thus far opened to him." D343

Still, Thénardier's deceit goes beyond acting and intention; it's in his bodily cells. He "looked ill but enjoyed excellent health, that was where his deceptiveness began." D341 Thénardier is two people, says Hugo, a man of cunning and a brute. He is poised, adroit at conniving on his feet, but to behold his fury is to gain "a glimpse of Hell." D1183 His concern for his family is solely to the extent he can use them. When he sends Eponine to Marius (their new neighbor in the dump next door) for a handout, Thénardier makes it clear, in the postscript to his letter, that the boy is welcome to his daughter for the price of whatever he can spare. Ordering his other daughter, Azelma, to smash her fist through a windowpane to heighten the impression of poverty, he's thrilled that her hand is bloodied, since it will elicit more pity from the about-to-visit potential benefactor Monsieur Fabre (a.k.a. Jean Valjean).

He claims to have studied for the priesthood and likes to be considered erudite, though his elegantly penned bills and letters contain spelling mistakes. He is a bit of a painter, too, and tries to sell Fabre-Valjean, at an exorbitant fee, the poorly painted sign that once fronted his inn — of a soldier, allegedly himself, carrying a wounded general to safety at the battle of Waterloo. [D677] His real action at Waterloo is selling provisions from a cart at a safe distance from the battle zone to those who actually did the fighting, then, when the combat is over, looting the corpses. The "saved general" — a captain promoted by Napoleon to colonel in the midst of the fighting at Waterloo — turns out to be Marius's father, who regains consciousness while Thénardier is stealing his ring, faints from the severity of his face wound, then wakes again from Thénardier's rough treatment as he steals his prey's silver cross of the Légion d'honneur. The colonel tries to give his watch and money purse as a reward to his "rescuer." Thénardier has already pocketed them. [D323-4]

### Eponine Thénardier

The famous aphorism of Hegel states: "Better a mended sock than a torn one. Not so with self-consciousness." Eponine is as torn as the rags that dress her malnourished, protruding bones. By dint of the squalid conditions of her life, by paternal treatment, she has every right to be her father. But it is part of the mystery of personality that the tear within her endows her with a profundity that he — and even Cosette and Marius — lack. When she appears, a total stranger, from behind a shrub of the old scholar Monsieur Mabeuf's garden and waters the beloved plants that starvation has rendered him too feeble to maintain on his own, he praises her as an angel. Eponine replies: "I'm no angel. I'm the devil, but it's all the same to me." [D750] It's a precise self-characterization. William Burroughs has said. "Now, some of you may encounter the devil's bargain if you get that far. Any old soul is worth saving, at least to a priest, but not *every* soul is worth buying — so you can take the offer as a compliment." By those standards Thénardier is a demon in whom the devil would have no interest. Eponine, part angel like Lucifer, deserves a shrine.

Eponine wants desperately to act from self-interest — and cannot, and can. This is her cross. It kills her in the end. It redeems and corrupts her, simultaneously, in equal measure, in the end. Eponine does not want to find out for Marius the address of the mysterious dream-girl whose name (Cosette) he does not yet know. She does. It wounds her that on the day of the disclosure he's not even glad to see her until the moment she announces she is in possession of the information he has coveted for more than a year. Having tracked down Cosette's house, having hunted out Marius for weeks to give him the news, up to the last second she seeks justification to withhold what she knows. "Oh well, it can't be helped," she says after biting her lip. "You look so miserable and I want you to be happy. But you must promise to smile."[D753] Marius grabs her hand, a touch she deeply longs for, demanding that Eponine take him there at once. Half of the girl's character Hugo divulges through a single, simple gesture: "She withdrew her hand and said in a tone of sadness that would have wrung the heart of any beholder, but of which Marius in his flurry was quite unconscious: 'Oh, how excited you are!'" [D754]

This same half of her, as they proceed to Cosette's residence, prompts Eponine to soon stop and warn: "You're keeping too close to me, Monsieur Marius. Let me walk on ahead and you must follow as though you didn't know me. It wouldn't do for a respectable young man like you to be seen in company with a woman of my kind." [D754] Hugo adds: "No words can convey the pathos of that word 'woman' spoken by that child." [D755]

### Two promises

Thus does Eponine advance the love of Marius and Cosette from fantasy to the real. Marius had promised his poor benefactress anything she wanted if she found the address but when they next meet six weeks later "the encounter gave him a shock. He had not given the girl a thought since the day she had led him to the Rue Plumet"[D852] (where Valjean and Cosette live under another name). His coldness to Eponine makes her run off. He sees her coming toward him the next day as well and turns off the street to avoid her. Hugo's explanation is worth noting: being in love, he says, far from perfecting a man, makes him forgetful. "If he forgets to be evil, he also forgets to be good." [D852]

Eponine follows the fleeing Marius to the Valjean house. He sneaks into the garden for his rendezvous with his darling; his shadow takes up "guard duty" on a hidden stoop, "her mind busy with thoughts." [D853-4] The demonic dimension of those thoughts we learn only later. The angelic aspect we learn now: the Thénardier gang has come to rob the place despite her earlier claim there was nothing in it to steal. Eponine defies them. "If you so much as touch this gate, I'll scream the place down. I'll rouse the whole neighborhood and have the lot of you pinched." [D856] She's known her whole life the truth of Hugo's warning about her pop: "A cool-headed knave," but "woe to those who ... fell foul of his wrath." [D342-3] Her sad, sad response to his threats: "I'm not scared ... Not even of you ... What do I care if my body's picked up in the street tomorrow morning, beaten to death by my own father — or found in a year's time in the ditches round Saint-Cloud ... along with the garbage and the dead dogs." [D857]

*"You know, Monsieur Marius, I think I was a little bit in love with you"*

Having saved, Eponine sets out to destroy. She swaps clothes with another urchin who thought it fun to dress up as a girl. She sneaks up from behind on Valjean — seated in disguise in a park — and drops a note in his lap that reads, "Clear Out!" Already alarmed that he had seen Thénardier several times prowling the neighborhood, further troubled that the political unrest in Paris made the police more obtrusive than the norm, having discovered that morning a mysterious address newly scrawled on his garden wall, Valjean informs Cosette they will leave France for England. Panicked, Cosette hurries off a note to Marius, telling him the terrible news, and that he is to come to her at another Paris address where she'll be only for a week before going abroad. Not allowed out of the house unchaperoned, she despairs of posting the letter, but spots a ragged boy pacing in front of her garden and hires him to do the job. Eponine has no intention of delivering the letter. Instead, driven by jealousy, she goes to the address on the envelope to see where her beloved lives. She learns from Marius's roommate Courfeyrac that their friends have built a barricade in the name of the lost ideals of the French Revolution. Eponine, discovering she's inherited her father's flair for dramatic plots, opts to use the barricade as the setting for Marius's death — and hers too. Following Courfeyrac so as to determine the location of the barricade, she returns to the garden of Valjean's house, certain Marius will go there as planned since she has pocketed the letter that would inform him his beloved has moved. She banks, correctly, on Marius's anguish at finding Cosette gone and the house vacated, and summons him, ostensibly in the name of his friends, to the barricade. He, as she knows he will, heads off to join his friends at once.

When Eponine, too, arrives at the barricade, her capacity for sacrifice surpasses even the love she bears Marius in the musical. During the fighting she puts her hand over the soldier's musket that will kill her beloved; the bullet goes through her chest and out her back. What's missing in the Eponine of the musical, however, the novel makes evident in her dying words to the man she saved:

> "You're finished. Nobody's going to get out of the barricade alive now. I'm the one who led you here, ha! You're going to die, I should damn well hope so. And yet, when I saw they were aiming at you,

I stuck my hand over the mouth of the gun barrel. Funny, isn't it! But it's only because I wanted to die before you did ... Do you remember the day I came into your room and I looked at myself in your mirror, and the day I ran into you on the boulevard [with the news she'd discovered Cosette's address]? ... You gave me a hundred sous, and I said to you: I don't want your money ... The sun was shining bright, we weren't cold for once. Do you remember, Monsieur Marius? Oh, I'm so happy! Everyone's going to die." R937

The sentence sequence is perfect in its ambiguity. "I'm so happy!" refers back to the only two occasions when Marius was warm to her, to her present ecstasy of her head finally resting on her beloved's lap, to her enraptured vision of a future near and far in which Marius — and the whole world — will die. She discloses to Marius that the letter is in her pocket, and finally asks for the payment he once promised if she found where Cosette lived: "You must kiss me on the forehead after I'm dead." D966

This he does: "a deliberate, tender farewell to an unhappy spirit." D966 Yet "scarcely had the poor unhappy girl closed her eyes than Marius was thinking about opening the note." R939 Hugo calls it the "nature of man." D966 The same contradictory nature of man that prompts him to first lay Eponine's corpse gently on the ground and move away "feeling instinctively that he could not read it beside her dead body."D966 The same human nature that assures us that Eponine's insistence that she saved Marius solely so she could die before him is — partly — a lie.

*"Bring him home" (with a touch of falsetto) — just not to **my** home (whispered in bass)*

Months earlier, Valjean had joyfully concluded that his fears over Marius from the previous summer — he did not know the interloper's name — had been a delusion. That the serpent was nightly entering his Eden he could not have conceived. He had optimistic plans for Cosette and himself in England, certain once more that she was, and would remain, only his.

But on the first night of the barricade, after Marius's grandfather refuses to lend him the money to follow her abroad, Valjean accidentally sees, reflected in the mirror, the imprint of Cosette's desperate letter to her lover on her ink blotter. It precipitates in the saintly Valjean a "spiritual collapse." [D975]

> Until that moment no trial had been too much for Jean Valjean. He had endured hideous ordeals; no extremity of ill-fortune had been spared him ... He had stood his ground unflinching, accepting, when he had to, the bitterest blows ... [He] seemed to have achieved the self-abnegation of a martyr. His conscience, fortified by so many battles with a malignant fate, had seemed unassailable ... Of all the torments he had suffered in his long trial by adversity, this was the worst. [D974]

It's a turning point in the novel, absent in the musical. The point at which the demands of justice cannot be relinquished in the name of love. Marius joins the barricade not primarily for politics but to die without Cosette. With the stakes so high, the injustice of Valjean's supreme love for his daughter borders on evil.

The reasons are understandable enough: "Jean Valjean had known nothing of the things that men love."[D974-5] The trusting child he had rescued touched him — to steal an image from Erich Maria Remarque — like a match to dry straw. "He loved Cosette as his daughter, his mother, his sister; and since he had neither mistress nor wife, since nature is a creditor who accepts no compromise, that kind of love, too, was mingled with the others." [D974]

Hugo writes that his re-incarceration — deleted in the musical — upon divulging his identity in court to save a falsely arrested man had just about broken Valjean. "He had been sent back to prison, this time for a good deed. Renewed bitterness had assailed him, disgust and weariness, to the point that even the sacred memory of the bishop was perhaps at moments eclipsed ... Who can be sure that Jean Valjean had not been on the verge of losing heart and giving up the struggle? In loving [Cosette] he recovered his strength." [D394]

Describing the early impact of Cosette on Valjean, Hugo makes this interesting remark: "The bishop had taught him the meaning of virtue; Cosette had now taught him the meaning of love." [D392] For Valjean virtue meant: following the commandment to love others as oneself even in the absence of emotion. *Love as will.* Cosette taught him *love as emotion.* But we all know that love as unchecked emotion is endangered: "The crushing evidence that another possessed her heart and was the end and purpose of her life, and that he was no more than a father, someone who no longer existed ... [unleashed] to the very roots of his hair an overweening rebirth of egotism." [D975] The infinitely loving singer of the prayerful "Bring Him Home" in the musical is not *all* he is. Panicked by his rival, "Jean Valjean, the man who had redeemed himself, who had mastered his soul and with such painful effort resolved all life, suffering, and hardship in love, turned his inward vision upon himself: and a ghost rose before his eyes — hatred." [D976]

He staggers outside and sits, stymied, on the curb that fronts his house. There he intercepts Gavroche's attempted delivery of Marius's letter to Cosette. He reads with shaking hand that, with their love doomed, Marius shall die on the barricade. Valjean "stared in a kind of drunken bemusement at the letter. There, beneath his eyes, was a marvel — the death of the hated person ... His problem was solved ... Valjean felt that he was saved ... He had only to keep the letter in his pocket." [D980-1]

Thirty minutes later, in his National Guard uniform, armed with a musket, he heads off to the barricade.

*Why Kierkegaard wrote a book warning "Purity of Heart is to Will One Thing"*

As the barricade is overrun by government troops, Marius receives yet another wound from a bullet to the shoulder but a hand seizes him as he falls — Jean Valjean's. Thus begins, with all the other insurrectionists dead, the celebrated escape through the sewers of Paris. The trudge through the "horrid excrement of the town,"[D1084] with an unconscious, barely-breathing body slung over his shoulder, is a feat that only a man of Valjean's strength and capacity for sacrifice could undergo. In the chapter called "He Too Bears His Cross," a shaft of light from a large hatchway gives him a place to finally rest the body momentarily. The sleepless, starving, rat-bitten Valjean sets it down "with the gentleness of a man handling a wounded brother." [D1085] Marius's arms droop limp; blood runs from the corners of his mouth. Tearing strips from his own shirt Valjean bandages the wounds as best he can. "Then, bending over the unconscious form in that dim light, he stared at him with inexpressible hatred." [D1085]

Exhausted, no longer certain Marius is alive, he sinks beneath the body into a quicksand-like pit of shit. "Only his head was now above water, and his two arms, carrying Marius ... He went on, tilting his face upwards so that he could continue to breathe. Anyone seeing him at that moment might have thought him a mask floating in the darkness." [D1088-9] His foot rests on something solid. Saved! — but not saved. He reaches a turning in the tunnel and sees in the distance the light of the Paris day. The grill obstructing the exit is locked. He is too out of strength to turn back. He prepares to die, thinking of Cosette. A voice says: "We'll go halves." [D1091] It's Thénardier, who continues: "You won't have killed that man without looking to see what he has in his pocket. Give me half and I'll unlock the door ... Want to see what a master key looks like?" [D1092]

Valjean doesn't notice that Thénardier has torn off and pocketed a fragment of Marius's coat.[1] The jackal, who does not recognize the slime-covered Jean Valjean, of course takes all of the little money Valjean had in his pocket when he left for the barricade. But Thénardier does unlock the gate. For the altruistic reason that he

---

[1] In the musical he removes Marius's ring.

knows that on the other side is the cop who'd been trailing him — Javert.

The last ever encounter of Valjean with Javert, and how Marius's body is taken to his grandfather, the reader will recall from Part Three.

### *The final driven nail*

"To be happy is a terrible thing," writes Hugo. "How complacent we are, how self-sufficing. How easy it is, being possessed of the false side of life, which is happiness, to forget the real side, which is duty." [D1173]

These words are written about Marius. They are, in fact, the divine poison that slay Jean Valjean.

> The question was this: how was he, Jean Valjean, to ensure the continued happiness of Cosette and Marius? It was he who had brought about this happiness ... But what was he about to do with it, this happiness that he had brought about? Should he take advantage of it, treat it as though it belonged to him? ... Could he, without saying a word, bring his past into that future? [D1142]

Prior to their wedding, Valjean retrieves his fortune of 600,000 francs, made in the glass jewelry business and buried in the forest years before. He gives the money to the couple, ensuring their financial freedom. His daughter and new family insist he live with them in the house of Marius's grandfather; Valjean had "almost promised"[D1130] to do so. Shortly before the wedding, however, faking injury, he wraps his arm in a sling to prevent him from signing the marriage documents. He sits hidden in a corner during the wedding party and leaves early — bothered by his injury, he says — without taking leave of Cosette.

What waits in his empty room is "mortal combat with his own conscience." [D1142] Must he, or can he not, tell Marius that he is not the philanthropist-gentleman Ultime Fauchelevent but Jean Valjean, a criminal even now in breach of parole. Hugo describes it as "a tempest fiercer than the one that had once driven him to [the courtroom in] Arras." [D1143] His dilemma, simply stated, is this: "Cosette, that exquisite creature, was his lifeline. Was he to cling to it or let it go? If he clung to it, then he was safe; he could go on living. But if he let it go … Then, the abyss." [D1143]

The nature of the bishop's mercy that redeemed Valjean meant he could be merciful to all but himself. For twelve hours, slumped over the tiny valise he always kept near him — containing the first dress, shoes, and stockings he'd bought for ragged Cosette — he tries to justify averting his destruction, "fists clenched and arms out-flung like those of a man cut down from the cross." The morning after the wedding night he confesses his identity to Marius, who for more pleasant reasons "too, had not slept all night." [D1146]

*"Once I stole a loaf of bread in order to stay alive; but now I cannot steal a name to go on living"*

Marius is stupefied by — and suspicious of — Valjean's declaration that he is an ex-con. Why didn't he keep his mouth shut? He hasn't been denounced; he isn't being pursued. There must be some hidden reason. Valjean divulges what it is:

Conscience is a strange thing. It would have been so easy to say nothing. I spent the whole night trying to persuade myself to do so ... I gave myself excellent reasons. But it was no use. I could not break that bond in my heart or silence the voice that speaks to me when I am alone ... To continue to be Monsieur Fauchelevent would have settled everything — except my conscience ... I should have been a figure of deceit, ... sitting at your table with the thought that if you knew who and what I was you would turn me out — the very servants would have exclaimed in horror! ... Cheating you day after day, my beloved, trusting children! ... I should never have ceased to be sickened by my own treachery and cowardice. [D1149-50]

Valjean dreads what it will mean for the couple if "one day, when we are talking and laughing, a voice cries 'Jean Valjean!' and the terrible hand of the police descends on my shoulder and strips the mask away!" [D1152] Marius dreads Cosette's reaction when she learns that the man she thought was her father is a felon. Cosette having to be told is the one element Valjean in his anguished meditation has failed to foresee. It's the one nail beyond his endurance and he exacts from Marius the promise to keep the secret from her. Valjean's final question: whether he should see Cosette no more, gets an icy response from Marius; it is better, he declares, if ex-father and daughter do not meet again. Valjean initially submits, then, pleading he would have nothing left to live for, begs Marius for permission to see Cosette from time to time. He won't stay long. They can meet in the ground-floor room used as a cellar. Marius relents, promising Valjean can meet her each evening, but soon repents this moment of weakness, agonized "that Cosette would still be in contact with the man." D1161

Marius, intentionally never at home during these visits, at first fails to arrange for the servants to clean out the spiders, dead flies, and empty bottles from the dilapidated room, though he does order a fire to be lit that at least reduces some of the chill. Cosette evidently complains, for the next evening the insects and bottles are gone, but soon there is no fire. Cosette again complains; next visit the fire returns, but the armchairs that she and Valjean sit in are pushed close to the door. One night later the chairs are missing. Valjean lies to Cosette that this is his idea but he never steps inside the house again.

Instead, clad in black, he walks each night to the intersection of the block on which Cosette lives. Trembling, tears falling, he "peered timidly round the corner into the street with the tragic expression of one who gazes into a forbidden paradise." D1171 It is this, after so many trials over so many decades, that breaks the inhuman strength of Jean Valjean. The distance he walks steadily decreases. One night he only gets as far as the curb in front of his house. The next night he cannot leave his room; the night after that, his bed. He stops eating. Gathering his last strength he tries to write a letter explaining how the 600,000 francs Marius won't touch (— he believes it tainted —) was honestly earned. In the chapter titled: "A Feather Crushes the Man Who Lifted Fauchelevent's Cart," Valjean has barely begun the letter when the quill pen slips from his shaking hand. "It's over," Valjean sobs. "I won't see her again ... Dying is nothing, what is unbearable is dying without seeing her. She would give me a smile, she would have a word with me. Would that hurt anyone?" [D1172]

## "The two candlesticks are made of silver, but to me they are pure gold"

From Thénardier's attempted bribe, Marius learns that Javert had not been murdered by Jean Valjean at the barricade but set free; that Valjean *was* Mayor Madeleine, therefore could not have robbed him of 600,000 francs; and — from the fragment of torn coat Thénardier presents him as proof Valjean is a murderer — that Valjean was the man who had carried him through the sewer and saved his life. As Marius and Cosette race by carriage to his home, as the ecstatic Thénardier is reveling in his 24,000-franc bonanza, Valjean, shattered and despondent, is dying.

The day of his confession to Marius he had said: "If you want to be happy you must have no sense of duty, because a sense of duty is implacable. To have it is to be punished, but it is also to be rewarded, for it thrusts you into a hell in which you feel the presence of God at your side." [D1150-1]

These words, for me, mark the final transformation of Valjean, his revised — and full — understanding of Luke 9: 24-26: ""If anyone would come after me, let him deny himself and take up his cross daily and follow me. For whoever would save his life will lose it, but whoever loses his life for my sake will save it." The reward of self-negation is not heaven but "a hell in which you feel the presence of God at your side." He confesses his error to

79

Cosette as part of the last paragraph he ever speaks: "You were so enchanting when you were small. You hung cherries over your ears. All those things are in the past — the woods we walked through, the convent where we took refuge, your child's eyes and laughter, all shadows now. I believed that it all belonged to me, and that is where I was foolish." [D1199]

Preferring to die rather than risk injury to Marius and Cosette by concealing his identity and becoming part of their household rids his capacity to love of every trace of egotism. There are, in the three scenes that push Valjean from dying to death, a simplicity and humility in him that are new, justifying fully Marius's characterization: "His courage, his saintliness, his selflessness, are beyond all bounds." [D1194] Valjean's kindly promise to the old concierge to eat for a change; his thanking Marius and Cosette for forgiving him as they charge into his room; his wistful comment — too late — that maybe Cosette's forbidding him to die means he won't have to; his admission to Marius: "I must confess that I have not always liked you, and I ask your forgiveness;" his request to be buried in any plot that is handy and that his gravestone bear no name; the innocence of his question as to whether the man who gave him the silver candlesticks he now bequeaths to Cosette is pleased with him, as well as his own meek answer: "I have done my best,"[D1199] — all contain a sweetness, even in his dying radiant delirium, that after so many re-readings, over so many years — still shakes me as I write.

# Cited Books

Bradley, A.C. *Shakespearean Tragedy*. London: Penguin Books, 1991.

Camus, Albert. *The Rebel*. Translated by Anthony Bower. Middlesex: Penguin Books, 1971. (See the chapter "The Rejection of Salvation," on Dostoevsky's *The Brothers Karamazov*.)

Dostoevsky, Fyodor. *The Brothers Karamazov*. Translated by Richard Pevear and Larissa Volokhonsky. New York: Farrar, Straus and Giroux, 1990.

Heschel, Abraham. *Who is Man?* Stanford: Stanford University Press, 1965.

Hugo, Victor. *Les Misérables*. Translated by Norman Denny. London: Penguin, 1982. Referenced as D.

Hugo, Victor. *Les Misérables*. Translated by Julie Rose. New York: Modern Library Paperback, 2009. Referenced as R.

Kafka, Franz. *The Trial*. Translated by Willa and Edwin Muir. New York: Schocken Books, 1974.

Kierkegaard, Søren. *Purity of Heart Is To Will One Thing*. Translated by Douglas V. Steere. New York: Harper Torchbook, 1956.

Maugham, W. Somerset. *The Razor's Edge*. New York: Vintage International, 2003.

Niebuhr, Reinhold. *The Irony of American History*. New York: Charles Scribner's Sons, 1952.

Wiesel, Elie. *Souls on Fire: Portraits and Legends of Hasidic Masters*. Translated by Miriam Wiesel. New York: Random House, 1972.

# Film versions of Les Misérables

Film adaptations are listed in http://en.wikipedia.org/
wiki/Category:Films_based_on_Les_Misérables and
in Arnaud Laster, *L'Avant-scène cinéma*, No. 438/439.
Selection of films presently available on DVD:

1934. Directed by Raymond Bernard with Harry Baur as
   Valjean. DVD: Criterion Collection, Eclipse series 4.

1935 & 1952. The 1935 version directed by Richard
   Boleslawski features Fredric March as Valjean and
   Charles Laughton as Javert. The 1952 film by Lewis
   Milestone has Michael Rennie as Valjean. 2 DVD set
   (black and white): 20th-century Fox.

1957. Directed by Jean-Paul Le Chanois, with Jean
   Gabin as Valjean. Dubbed DVD version: Unicorn.

1972. French TV film in two parts directed by Marcel
   Bluwal with Georges Chéret as Jean Valjean. 2 DVD
   set: Ina Edition (no English subtitles).

1978. Two-part BBC series directed by Glenn Jordan
   featuring Richard Jordan as Valjean and Anthony
   Perkins as Javert. ITC Entertainment / Key Video.
   Several other VHS and DVD versions of this film cut
   half an hour or more of the original.

1982. French film directed by Robert Hossein with Lino
   Ventura as Valjean. DVD with French and English
   subtitles: L.C.J. Editions & Productions, 2000.

1998. Written by Rafael Yglesias, directed by Bille
   August, with Liam Neeson as Valjean. DVD: Sony
   Pictures Home Entertainment.

2000. French TV film series in four parts directed by
   Josée Dayan featuring Gérard Depardieu as Jean
   Valjean. DVD: TF1 Video.

*Further reading and viewing on the relationship
between selflessness, love and justice*

Dostoyevsky, Fyodor. *The Idiot*. Translated by Henry
    and Olga Carlisle. New York: Signet Classic,
    1969. (The unconditional love of the Christ-like
    Prince Myshkin transcends justice, with disastrous
    consequence.)

Fischer, Louis. *Gandhi and Stalin: Two Signs at the
    World's Crossroads*. New York: Harper and Brothers
    Publishers, 1947. (See chapter five, "We Are All
    Victims," 45-53, for Gandhi's troubling suggestion
    the European Jews during Hitler's reign should have
    committed mass suicide.)

Niebuhr, Reinhold. *Love and Justice: Selections from the
    Shorter Writings of Reinhold Niebuhr*. Edited by D.B.
    Robertson. Louisville: Westminster/John Knox Press,
    1957.

Niebuhr, Reinhold. *The Nature and Destiny of Man: A
    Christian Interpretation*. Volume New York: Charles
    Scribner's Sons, 1953. (For Niebuhr's discussion
    of love and justice see volume II: *Human Destiny*,
    chapter IX, "The Kingdom of God And The Struggle
    For Justice," 244-286.)

Orwell, George. *The Collected Essays, Journalism and
    Letters of George Orwell*. Edited by Sonia Orwell and
    Ian Angus. New York: Harcourt Brace Jovanovich,
    1968. (See "Reflections on Gandhi" in Volume IV
    [1945-50]: *In Front of Your Nose*, 463-470, for
    Orwell's profound critique of Gandhi's attempt to
    relate spirituality to justice. Includes Orwell remarks

on Gandhi's advocacy of mass Jewish suicide discussed in Louis Fischer's *Gandhi and Stalin*, listed above.)

Singer, Isaac Bashevis. *The Collected Short Stories of Isaac Bashevis Singer*. New York: Farrar, Straus, and Giroux, 1982. (For two very different treatments of the problematic relationship between love and justice see Singer's terrific stories "Gimpel the Fool," 3-14 and "The Manuscript," 525-532.)

Tillich, Paul: *Love, Power, and Justice*. Oxford: Oxford University Press, 1954.

## Films

*Camelot*. Book and Lyrics by Alan Jay Lerner. Music by Frederick Lowe. Warner Brothers. 1967. DVD: Burbank, CA: Warner Home Video, 1998. (King Arthur creates Camelot on the principle of justice, and destroys it by his inability to exact justice on the three people he loves, Guenevere, Lancelot, and his bastard son Mordred. Based on T.H. White's novel *The Once and Future King*.)

*El Topo*. Directed by and starring the Chilean-French filmmaker Alejandro Jodorowsky. 1970. DVD release: Troy, Michigan: Starz/Anchor Bay Home Video, 2007. (The second half of the film is a disturbing meditation on the relationship between love, power, and justice. A monk's loving—or self-loving?— attempt to bring justice to an oppressed community leads to their demise. Violent, and often perverse, but profound.)

# Index of Person's Names